Buzz Off!

600 Jokes About Things With Wings

Natasha Wing

STERLING CHILDREN'S BOOKS
New York

To my husband, Dan,

who gave me a Wing to fly on

—N. W.

STERLING CHILDREN'S BOOKS
New York

An Imprint of Sterling Publishing Co., Inc.
1166 Avenue of the Americas
New York, NY 10036

ISBN 978-1-4549-3196-6

Distributed in Canada by Sterling Publishing Co., Inc.
c/o Canadian Manda Group, 664 Annette Street
Toronto, Ontario M6S 2C8, Canada
Distributed in the United Kingdom by GMC Distribution Services
Castle Place, 166 High Street, Lewes, East Sussex BN7 1XU, England
Distributed in Australia by NewSouth Books
University of New South Wales, Sydney, NSW 2052, Australia

For information about custom editions, special sales, and premium
and corporate purchases, please contact Sterling Special Sales at
800-805-5489 or specialsales@sterlingpublishing.com.

Manufactured in Canada

Lot #:
2 4 6 8 10 9 7 5 3 1

08/19

sterlingpublishing.com

Cover design and illustration by Julie Robine
Interior design by Julie Robine

For Photo/Image credits, see page 96

HA HA HA HA HA HA Contents

DUCK, DUCK, GOOSE

What do you call a mallard with tires?

A rubber duckie.

Why did the duck get in trouble in school?

Because he used fowl language.

Why do geese make great Air Force pilots?

Because they fly in formation.

What did the goose say to the lead goose
in formation?

"I'll be your wingman!"

How did the policeman catch the duck?

He used a decoy.

What game do deer, mallards, and geese play?

Buck-Duck-Goose.

What did the goose say when a mallard came in for
a landing?

"Duck!"

Knock, knock.

> Who's there?

Waddle.

> Waddle who?

Waddle you do without me?

What time do ducks get up in the morning?

> At the quack of dawn!

What do you call crazy geese?

> Bonker honkers.

What do you get when you cross a match and a duck?

> Firequackers!

Where do ducks go to look up information?

> The World Wide Web.

Why did the ducks laugh when the goose landed?

> Its fly was down.

CAN YOU SAY THIS FIVE TIMES FAST?

> The goose has no loose tooth to lose.

HAHAHAHA

HA HA HA HA HA HA HA HA HA HA HA HA HA HA HA HA

Mallard and Swan were at a restaurant when Mallard got a phone call. He told Swan, **"I'm going to duck out for a moment."**

What did the goose say when it was offered a comforter to sleep on?
"I'm down with that!"

What's the worse kind of duck to be in an open pond?
A sitting duck!

What do you call a feisty duck covered in mud?
A plucky mucky ducky.

DUCK: Did you hear that Honker escaped? That goose is cooked!
SWAN: And you're a dead duck for telling on him!

Why did Mr. and Mrs. Goose order the same food?
What's good for the goose is good for the gander.

What do you call a goose on a cracker?
Pâté.

What did the gander bring to the potluck?

Gooseberry pie.

What's a duck's favorite movie treat?

Quacker Jacks.

How do you get down from a horse?

You don't! You get down from a goose. You get hair from a horse.

SWAN: How many fish does it take to paddle a boat?

DUCK: I don't know. How many?

SWAN: None! Fish don't paddle!

DUCK: You quack me up!

What do police call a goose that's escaped its jail cell?

A loosey goosey!

What happens when you read scary stories to a waterbird?

It gets goose bumps.

Why don't ducks use credit cards?

They'd rather pay in bills.

HA HA HA HA HA HA

Why don't ducks ever get upset?

They let things roll off of them like water off a duck's back.

Why don't geese freeze in the winter?

They wear down coats.

Why were the ducks always in debt?

They had a lot of bills.

What do you get when you cross a comedian with a bird?

A silly goose.

Why wasn't the farmer ready to build a new barn?

He had to get his ducks in a row.

What did the duck say when it waddled into a surprise party?

"You could have knocked me down with a feather!"

What's the duck's favorite song?

"Sittin' by the Duck on the Bay."

What did the pilot say to his co-pilot?
"Straighten up and fly right."

- -

Why was the plane so tired?
It had jet lag.

- -

Why did the cardinal get cut from the baseball team?
He always flew out.

- -

Why do birds fly south for the winter?
To get some antifreeze.

- -

Why is it easy to pick up a bird?
Because it is as light as a feather.

- -

Why did the tropical bird fly through the stoplight?
It was a flamin*go*!

- -

Why do birds migrate?
They do it out of habitat.

- -

CAN YOU SAY THIS FIVE TIMES FAST?
Three things with wings.

What do mama birds and older mothers have in common?

They both become empty nesters.

How do scarecrows give directions?

As the crow flies.

Why do geese fly south?

Because it's quicker than taking the bus.

Can cats ever get a bird's-eye view?

Why was the bird sneezing?

It had the flew.

Where do birds learn how to fly?

At flight school!

Why did the bird have trouble landing on the pond?

There was a flight log in its path.

How do birds know where to migrate?

Navigational pull.

HA HA HA
HA HA HA

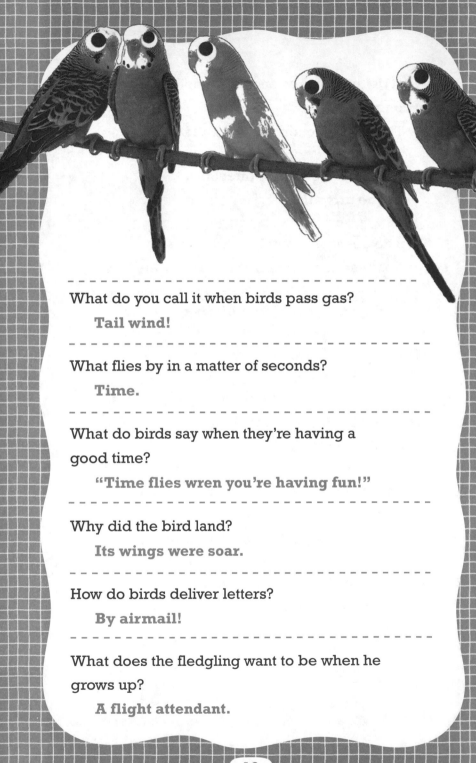

What do you call it when birds pass gas?

Tail wind!

What flies by in a matter of seconds?

Time.

What do birds say when they're having a good time?

"Time flies wren you're having fun!"

Why did the bird land?

Its wings were soar.

How do birds deliver letters?

By airmail!

What does the fledgling want to be when he grows up?

A flight attendant.

What did the mother bird say to her misbehaving baby bird?

"You'd better change your altitude!"

Overheard at the bird feeder:

"How did you find out I was flying south?"

"A little bird told me."

How do baby birds build up muscles to fly the nest?

They egg-cersize!

What do you get when you cross a falcon and a vehicle?

A hovercraft!

Where do birds book their travel plans?

On Cheepflights!

Why does the author of this book have trouble flying?

She only has one Wing.

What did the chick say when it saw the price of eggs?

"Cheep! Cheep!"

Why didn't the hen jump off the fence?

She chickened out!

What's the rooster's favorite legume?

The chickpea!

What's the hen's favorite gum?

Chick-lets!

What kind of cookies did the bird bake?

Chocolate cheep.

Why did the chicken squawk?

Because it got goosed.

Why did the chicken cross the road?

Because the school crossing guard told him to.

Why did the fox sit on the other side of the road?

To catch all the crossing chickens!

What do you call a chicken car seat?

A rooster booster!

What was the hen's favorite game to play?

Cluck-Cluck-Goose!

Where do farmers grow chickens?

On poul-trees!

What bugs do roosters eat?

Cockroaches!

What's the rooster's favorite cookie?

Snicker doodle do!

When is a chicken a teacher?

When it grades its eggs!

Why was it so hard for the policeman to get the chicken to confess?

It was a cagey bird.

What did the detective say when he investigated the chicken coop?

"Something smells fowl in here."

What do you get when you cross a rooster and an artist?

Cocka-doodler-do!

Frugal chickens only book cheep flights.

Why did the rooster stop getting invited to his friend's house?

All he wanted to do was play Chicken.

What do you get when you cross a chicken and a bison?

Buffalo wings!

What is the baby chick's favorite Easter candy?

Peeps!

Why are chickens good bakers?

They make all their cakes from scratch.

HA HA HA HA HA HA HA HA HA HA HA HA HA HA HA HA

What do you get when you cross a legume and a rooster?

A peacock.

What do you call a scared lunch?

A chicken sandwich!

NEIGHBOR BIRD: Where did your baby go?
MOTHER BIRD: He flew the coop!

TEACHER: I can't read your handwriting.
CHICKEN: Why not?
TEACHER: It's chicken scratch!

PICK THIS PECK:
**How many hens could a henpeck peck,
if a henpeck could peck hens?**

What do you call an attractive rooster?

A chick magnet.

What kind of lottery tickets do chickens buy?

Scratchers!

What do you get when you cross a chicken with clay?

A brick layer!

What did Chicken Little do when he was arrested?

He cried fowl.

What did the chicken say when it lost all its feathers?

"Just my pluck!"

Where do chickens connect with their friends?

On Facebawk.

How do chickens like their eggs?

Laid!

How often do chickens lay eggs?

Now and hen.

BIRD BRAINS

How do owls call their friends?

On a smartphone.

What do you call a stubborn whip-poor-will?

A whip-poor-won't.

What do you call a negative pelican?

A peli-can't.

Why did the dodo bird fail the test?

He was a birdbrain.

CAN YOU SAY THIS FIVE TIMES FAST?

Teeny Finnish finches finish first.

Where do crazy birds go?

To the loony bin!

What kind of bird gets sad in the winter?

Bluebirds.

What do seabirds do when they can't get to sleep?

Toss and tern!

Why did the bird spell "goo" instead of "go"?

It had a sparrow.

CAN YOU SAY THIS FIVE TIMES FAST?

Seven startling starlings started staring.

Why did the crow go crazy?

It was stark raven mad!

What do you call a seabird that keeps coming back?

A re-tern!

What did the bird say when the teacher asked for volunteers?

"Peck me! Peck me!"

Where do owls go to learn?

Night school! And if owl else fails, there are online classes.

What do you get when you cross Minnesota's state bird with a small arachnid?

A loon-a-tick!

HA HA

Why do birds fly into windows?

Because they're flighty.

What do you call a clumsy bird?

A whoopsie crane!

Knock-knock!

Who's there?

Parrot.

Parrot who?

Parrot who?

What do you get when you cross a lamp and a bird?

A light as a feather.

- -

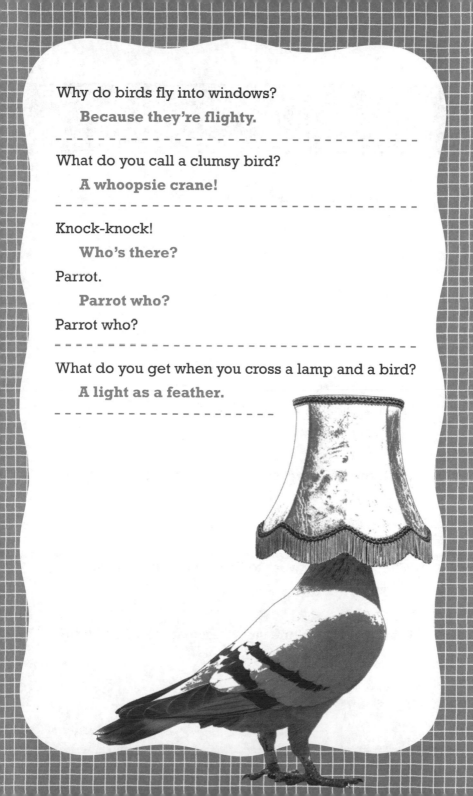

WORDS OF PREY

Why did the eagle wear a wig?

It was bald!

Knock, knock.

Who's there?

Talon.

Talon who?

I'm talon you to stop asking questions!

What do eagles serve on toast?

Wing spread.

What did the hawk say before it swooped down on its food?

"Prey for me."

What do eagles wear to fly in when it's cold out?

Thermal underwear.

What did the vulture say when it ate fresh roadkill?

"Hot off the grill!"

HA HA HA HA HA

HA HA HA HA HA HA HA HA HA HA

What kind of cookies do falcons like?

Orioles!

What do you call a bad-smelling bird dryer?

A foul owl towel!

A golden eagle went to a barbershop for a trim.

The barber buzzed all the feathers off his head.

"What did you do? Where are my feathers?"

The barber said,

"Now you're a bald eagle!"

OWL: Vultures will never eat dead clowns.

HAWK: Why?

OWL: Because they taste funny!

What do vultures eat for dessert?

Magpies!

GIRL OWL: Do you love me?

BOY OWL: Owl-ways!

CAN YOU SAY THIS FIVE TIMES FAST?

Cresting kestrels crashing.

What did the road kill say to the vulture?

"You want a piece of me?"

How did the bird make money?

He hawked his goods.

Knock-knock!

Who's there?

Owl.

Owl who?

Owl be right back!

Who is smarter than an owl?

A spelling bee!

What do you call an owl that just uses A, E, I, O, U, and sometimes Y?

A V'owl!

Which owl loves to ski?

The snowy owl.

Why do hawks, vultures, and eagles go to church?

They are birds of pray.

HA HA HA

HA HA HA HA HA HA HA HA

What's the buzzard's favorite winter sport?

Hawk-ey.

Who did the owl call when it needed a lawyer?

A legal eagle!

Why did the owl skip choir practice?

He didn't give a hoot!

Which bird should you invite to Thanksgiving dinner?

The turkey vulture.

What kind of bird chops wood?

A tomahawk!

What football team do birds of prey root for?

Eagles!

What sporting event do night birds like to watch?

The Owl-ympics!

What did one turkey vulture say to another?

"Buzzard off!"

VULTURE: Nothing gets past Baldy.

FALCON: He's got an eagle eye.

What kind of luggage do vultures take on board?

Carrion!

- -

Why did the vulture cross the road?

To eat the chicken that didn't make it to the other side.

- -

Which night owl loves scary movies?

The screech owl!

- -

Which owl pitches hay?

The barn owl!

- -

VULTURE: Who's making all that racket this late at night?

FALCON: Must be the night owls.

- -

How did the owl figure out how far to fly?

It used owl-gebra!

- -

What do you get when you cross a rabbit and a night bird?

A burrowing owl!

- -

HA HA HA HA HA HA HA HA HA HA

Knock-knock!

   Who's there?

Carrion.

   Carrion who?

Carrion with what you were doing.

What do you call it when an owl takes a poop?

   A b'owl movement!

   CAN YOU SAY THIS FIVE TIMES FAST?

   Blizzard buzzard.

Golden Opportunity: Do golden eagles lay golden eggs?

Knock-knock!

   Who's there?

Owl.

   Owl who?

Owl say it again.

How many cans do you need to make a bird?

Toucans!

What infection do flamingoes get?

Pink eye!

What's the tropical bird's favorite
Disney World ride?

Parrots of the Caribbean.

CAN YOU SAY THIS FIVE TIMES FAST?

Forty favorite famous flamingos.

PARROT: I swear, officer, I'm telling the truth.

OFFICER: I'll need you to take a Polly-graph to
prove it.

Knock-knock!

Who's there?

Macaw.

Macaw who?

Macaw the police!

HA HA HA HA HA

What did the sparrow say to the parrot?

"Talk is cheep!"

Knock-knock.

Who's there?

Parrot.

Parrot who?

Parrot who?

Parrot who who?

Parrot who who?

Why do birds like tennis?

Toucan play that game.

What sport do lovebirds watch?

Tennis, because of the scoring
(15-Love, 30-Love, 40-Love).

What the flamingo's favorite singer?
   Pink!

Why do flamingos have lots of parties?
   They like to fla-mingle.

Flamingoes have a leg to stand on.

Where do songbirds go on vacation?
   The Canary Islands.

Where do parrots go on vacation?
   The Polly-nesian Islands.

How do lovebirds kiss?
   They give each other pecks on the cheek.

What toothpaste do peacocks use?
   Crest.

Where do peacocks shop for new tail feathers?
   At the re-tail store.

HA HA HA

SEABIRD SILLIES

What do you call a pelican that's eaten too much?

A belly-can!

Where do pelicans store loose change?

In their pouch.

Where do pelicans learn how to catch fish?

Diver's ed.

When does a bird smell like a fish?

When it sits on a perch.

What did one seabird say to the other seabird when he asked her to marry him?

"One good tern deserves another."

Which ocean bird has great eyesight?

The see-gull.

When is the best time for seabirds to catch crabs on the beach?

When the tide has terned.

Knock-knock!
> Who's there?

Puffin.
> Puffin who?

Puffin so hard since I ran all the way here.

What pirate can fly?
> Jack Sparrow.

What's the pirate's favorite football team?
> Seattle Seahawks.

What did the mama seagull tell the baby seagull when papa flew out to sea?
> "Wave!"

Why are seabirds so confident?
> They are very shore of themselves.

Knock-knock!
> Who's there?

Heron.
> Heron who?

I'm heron your doorstep!

Where do seagulls ride on ships?
On the poop deck!

What bird would you smear with cream cheese?
A bay gull!

Who visits good buoys and gulls on
Christmas Eve?
Sandy Claws.

Knock-knock!
Who's there?
Osprey.
Osprey who?
Osprey for you!

What did the heron say when he couldn't catch up?
"Wade for me!"

How do you know when a seabird is out of breath?

It's puffin.

- -

What kind of bikes do seagulls ride?

Coast-ers!

- -

Why don't birds stay buddies for very long?

They are fair-feather friends.

- -

Why are seabirds great to tell jokes to?

They are so *gull*ible!

NESTER JESTERS

Why did the bird build a nest?

She was told to go lay an egg.

- -

Why did the baby bird move to a bigger tree?

He wanted to branch out.

- -

Where do birds sleep?

In feather beds.

- -

Why are birds good nest builders?

Because they studied carpen-tree.

How do birds clean their nests?

With feather dusters.

What did the mama bird say to her babies?

"If you're good, I'll give you some tweets!"

What game does a mama bird play with her baby bird?

Beakaboo!

How could you tell the bird store owner was successful?

He opened a lot of branches.

What kind of books do birds read in bed?

Mys-trees!

What do birds say when they go out for Halloween?

"Twig or tweet!"

Where do birds save their money?

In a nest egg.

Why did the baby bird leave the nest?

He didn't want to be a bird-en.

HA HA HA HA HA

What do nests and unwanted salesmen have in common?

They both stick around.

What do birds like to recite?

Poetree!

Sign on a bird nest: Home Tweet Home

Sign on a bird nest: Good things come in trees.

Why was the bird so serious about making money?

Because he was earnest.

How did the birds make their home fancy?

They feathered their nest.

Do nuthatches hatch nuts?

CARDINAL TO BLUE JAY: You have lots of relatives!

BLUE JAY: I have a big family tree.

What math are birds good at?

Twigonometry!

Where do birds like to do business?

In dis tree.

What do you call a bird that lies?

Disho*nest*.

How did the doctor put the bird asleep?

With a*nesth*esia!

What did the egg say when it fell out of the nest?

"That's how I roll!"

SING ALONG

Which bird plays a musical instrument?

A trumpeter swan!

Which little bird loves to sing along?

The hummingbird!

Why did the canaries get married?

They were tweethearts.

What did the catbird get arrested for?
    Prowling!

Why did the bird sing every hour?
    Because it was cuckoo.

Where do owls go to sing and dance?
    The *hoot*enanny!

Which bird meows?
    A catbird!

What's another name for "The Owl and
the Pussycat"?
    "Puss 'n Hoots"!

Why do woodpeckers like heavy metal music?
    Because they're headbangers!

How do geese tell you to get out of the way?
    They honk!

    Do songbirds take notes?

**HA HA HA HA HA
HA HA HA HA HA HA HA HA
HA HA HA HA HA**

RE-TWEET THIS: How many tweets can a twitter tweet, if a twitter could tweet tweets?

Knock-knock!

Who's there?

Tern.

Tern who?

Tern up the volume so I can hear the music!

What do you get when you cross a hummingbird and a guitar?

A strumming bird.

Why did the bird join the opera?

It was a warbler.

What do you get when you cross a black-capped songbird with a legume?

A chicka-pea.

What did the warbler have for a treat after she lost all her feathers?

A chocolate molt.

What did the songbird tell his music teacher?

I forgot my notes.

Why was the songbird sent to the principal's office?

He was always in treble.

What woodwind instrument do birds play?

The clari*nest*.

How did the birds feel when they got a new computer?

They were all atwitter.

How do birds send messages?

They tweet!

What do birds do when they like a Twitter post?

They re-tweet it!

What did The Byrds sing at their final performance?

A swan song.

What bird plays in an orchestra?

A horned owl!

What do you call a hilarious joke from a hummingbird?

A humdinger.

HA HA HA HA HA HA HA HA

Which cartoon character is hard to get off social media?

Tweety Bird.

- -

What do you call a yellow bird that won't sing?

A can't-ary!

- -

How much did the bird pay for its birdhouse?

It got it for a song!

NO-FLY ZONE

Where do ostriches live?

In no-fly zones.

- -

Why would penguins make great baseball players?

Because they never fly out.

- -

What do you call goofy penguins?

Frosted flakes!

- -

Which bird would rather drive than fly?

The roadrunner!

- -

How do emus measure how far they've traveled?

In feet!

How do penguins see the world?

In black-and-white.

- -

Who rules the Antarctic?

The emperor penguin!

- -

What did the explorer say when he saw the penguin take off its jacket?

"The emperor has no clothes!"

- -

Why did the bird get kicked out of the band?

It kept asking, "What kiwi in?"

- -

Which bird has a lot of money?

The ost-rich!

- -

What happens to black-and-white penguins during global warming?

They turn gray.

How do queen bees style their hair?

With a honeycomb!

What does a bee say when someone pesters it for information?

"None of your buzz-ness!"

Where do bees go to the bathroom?

In the honey pot-ty!

CAN YOU SAY THIS FIVE TIMES FAST?

Which wasp was walking?

GIVE ME A BUZZ: How many bees could a buzzing bee buzz, if a buzzing bee could buzz bees?

Why are bees good at finding seashells?

Because they love to comb the beach.

What did the bee say to the pesky hornet?

"Buzz off!"

HA HA HA

What do you get when you cross the Terminator and a bee?

The Pollinator.

- -

How many letters are in the insect alphabet?

One: *bee!*

- -

How do bees find their queen?

They send out drones.

- -

What does the mama bee call her baby?

Honey.

- -

How do bees make bread?

With flower.

- -

What's the bee's favorite band?

Queen.

- -

What kind of movie did the bumblebees see?

A B movie!

- -

What did the bumblebees do when the movie was over?

Made a beeline for the door!

- -

SHAKESPEARE FOR INSECTS: To bee, or not to bee, that is the question.

What did the bumblebee say to his girlfriend on Valentine's Day?

"Honey, will you bee mine?"

What is the insects' favorite basketball team?

The Hornets!

What do hornets drive?

Corvette Stingray!

What do balding men and bees have in common?

They both have comb-overs!

Which bees never stop to play?

Worker bees!

Where do bees live?

In Poli-nation.

What do you get when you take a bee out of bowl?

Owl!

Why are wasps good at catching thieves?

Because they can set up a sting.

Why did the police arrest the insect?

Because it was a killer bee.

What do you call a hornet that sings?

A stinger singer.

How did the wasp-control man remove the wasp nest?

Very carefully!

What's the bumblebee's favorite motto?

Bee yourself.

Why did the girl make everyone mad?

Because she stepped in a hornet's nest.

- -

What's the bee's favorite piano song?

"Flight of the Bumblebee."

- -

What did the bumblebee eat for lunch?

A bee-nut butter and honey sandwich.

QUIT BUGGING ME!

Why did the boy douse the bugs with waterr?

They were fireflies!

- -

What did the angry driver say to the firefly?

"Turn off your blinkers!"

- -

Knock-knock!

Who's there?

Locust.

Locust who?

Locust, so wash his mouth out with soap!

- -

Why did the ladybug blush?

Because it was spotted kissing.

HA HA HA HA HA HA HA HA

What bug loves to sing?

Ladybug Gaga.

What insect can tell the weather?

Lightning bugs!

What do you get when you cross a pest and a burrito?

Mosquito!

Where do pesky insects go on vacation?

The Mosquito Coast in Nicaragua.

What bug is best to be around on cold winter days?

A firefly!

How do you make the butterfly?

Throw the butter dish.

What do you call an arrogant insect thief?

A smug bug thug.

What bug is easy to catch, and the only way to throw it is up?

A stomach bug!

HA HA HA

HA HA HA HA HA

What do termites do for good luck?
They lock on wood!

What do you get when you cross a termite and a log?
Sawdust!

Gender bender: Can a ladybug be male?

What insect do you give on Valentine's Day?
A lovebug!

What holiday do moths celebrate?
Moth-er's Day!

Why don't insects own phones?
Because they don't want to be bugged.

What kind of insect do you put on toast?
Butterflies!

Do ants fly?
Ter-might!

What insects taste good barbecued?
Mesquite-oes.

What happens when locusts eat a telephone pole?

They create an electrical swarm.

Where do moths go to dance?

To the mothball!

What do you get when you cross the lawn
with a frog?

Grasshopper!

How do butterflies get television reception?

Through their antennae!

What do toads put on toast?

Butter-flies.

What's the moth's favorite drink?

An iced cold Porch Light.

What do termites say when you ask them a
question?

"I'll chew on that."

What happens when locusts gather in the winter?

A snow-swarm!

HA HA HA HA HA

What's the insects favorite cartoon character?

Bugs Bunny.

- -

What bugs do you find in bathrooms?

Stinkbugs!

- -

Why did the bug go to the doctor?

Because it was a cicada.

FLYING MAMMALS

What transportation do bats take when they don't want to fly?

Batmobile.

- -

One pig to another: They used to say, "When elephants fly" until Dumbo came along.

- -

BULLWINKLE: What happened? Did you crash?

ROCKY: I got off to a rocky start.

- -

What do you get when you cross a bird and a horse?

Pegasus!

What do you get when you cross a mustang with a pest?

A horsefly!

- -

Chase me: Do bird dogs chase catbirds?

- -

What do you get when you cross a nutty kingfisher and a donkey?

A kookaburro!

- -

Which reindeer delivers presents on Valentine's Day?

Cupid!

- -

What's hairy, has tusks, and flies?

A mam-moth!

Where do bats pee?

In the bat-room.

Knock-knock!

Who's there?

Guano.

Guano who?

Guano go to the park with me?

Why did the bat go to the doctor?

He had a bug.

Why did Quasimodo go to the doctor?

Because he had bats in the belfry.

What game do bats like to play?

Baseball.

And how did the coach know flying mammals would be good baseball players?

He knew right off the bat!

Why do flying mammals make good friends?

They'll go to bat for you!

How do nocturnal mammals fly so long?

They're bat-tery powered.

HA HA HA HA HA HA HA HA

What's black-and-white and flies?

Peter Pan-da.

What carries its own trunk when it flies?

Dumbo!

What did one bat say to another when their friend bumped into a wall?

"He's as blind as a bat!"

What do you call a group of cowbirds?

A herd!

What kind of canine can fly?

A bird-dog!

What bats avoid garlic?

Vampire bats!

What do you call Rudolph flying through a storm?

A rain deer.

What did the Wizard of Oz say when he saw Dorothy?

"Well, I'll be a flying monkey's uncle!"

READY FOR TAKE-OFF

Pilots are just plane people with a special air about them.

- -

BOY TO AIRPLANE PILOT: Being a pilot must be exciting!
PILOT: Not if I do it right.

- -

A girl was going to ride on a small plane
but there wasn't enough room for both of
her parents to come with her.
Her mother asked her daughter,
"If you can have only one other person on the
plane with you, who do you want it to be?"
"The pilot!"

- -

What happens when an airplane flies through a storm over Spain?
The rain in Spain falls mainly on the plane.

- -

Why did the pilots blush?
They saw the landing strip.

- -

HAHAHAHAHA

Which television shows do plane fliers like best?

Pilot episodes.

AIR TRAFFIC CONTROLLER TO SMALL PLANE PILOT: Are you ready for takeoff?
PILOT: Not jet!

Where do roosters sit on planes?

The cockpit.

What has a propeller but can't fly?

A beanie hat!

How do fashion designers pilot planes?

They fly by the seat of their pants.

What do you get when you cross a Boeing 747 with a 777?

580,419 (747 x 777).

Why don't chickens book nonstop flights?

They need a layover.

Pilots make decisions on the fly.

How do you ship an automobile?

On a cargo plane.

How do pilots send messages?

Paper airplanes!

Why couldn't the flight attendant fly?

She had cabin fever.

What kind of hairstyle do pilots sport?

A crew cut.

What's the helicopter pilot's favorite movie?

Blade Runner.

Why did the girl bring a clock on the plane?

She wanted to see time fly!

INVENTOR: I'm going to pitch an idea for a new flying machine to the boss.

ASSISTANT: It'll never fly.

Why are pilots big dreamers?

They always have their heads in the clouds.

Why did the pilot almost choke?

He had to wait until his airway was cleared.

What do you get when you cross a helicopter and an artist?

Helicopter sketch pad.

Which airline do explorers fly?

Frontier.

What did the pirate shout when the airplane was descending?

"Land-ho!"

Misdirection: Can you fly north or east on Southwest Airlines?

GRANDMA: I flew all the way from Florida to see you.

GRANDSON: Your arms must be sore!

HA HA HA
HA HA HA

GRANDSON: Where did all the planes go?
GRANDMA: They fleeted!

How did the mechanic attach the flap to the wing?

With wing nuts.

What did the trainer say to the graduating pilot?

"You're on the flight path to success!"

What plane makes a good housekeeper?

A crop duster!

What do you call a dent in a plane's wing?

A wingding.

Why did the flight attendant have to double-check the passenger list?

Because the Rumors were flying!

OUT OF THIS WORLD

What do you call the Toy Story character when his flight suit shrinks?

Buzz Tightgear.

- -

What brand of gum do astronauts chew?

Orbit.

- -

What did the astronauts say to the taxi driver?

"Can you give me a liftoff?"

- -

Astronauts are so spacey.

- -

What do astronauts say in crowds?

"Can you give me some space?"

- -

If the early bird gets the worm, what does an early astronaut get?

The wormhole!

- -

Why did the rocket fizz?

Because it soda ran out of fuel.

- -

What hot beverage do astronauts drink?

Gravi-tea.

Where do you read about astronauts who die?

In the orbit-uaries.

What do astronauts like in their sandwiches?

Launch meat.

What's an astronaut's favorite dessert?

Moon pies!

How do astronauts get from their house to the airport?

They take the space shuttle.

Knock-knock.

Who's there?

Fuel.

Fuel who?

Fuel you once, I'll fuel you again.

What's a young scientist's favorite subject at school?

Arts and spacecrafts.

HA HA HA HA HA HA HA HA HA

Why are astronauts so fast?

Because they're light-years ahead.

What do astronauts wear to business meetings?

Space suits.

Why are astronauts excellent at everything?

Because they go above and beyond.

Why did the astronaut fail the test?

He was under a lot of atmospheric pressure.

What social media do astronauts use?

Spacebook.

What kind of computers do astronauts have?

Launchpads.

Why did the astronaut go to the doctor?

He was airsick.

How do astronomers clean their bathrooms?

With Comet!

Why do rocket scientists live out in the country?

They need the space.

Why did the girl become an astronaut?

Her teacher told her to reach for the stars.

How do astronauts know they are attracted to one another?

Gravitational pull.

Why don't you see astronauts working out at the gym?

Because they are weightless.

How does Santa deliver presents to astronauts?

By Comet!

What rocket is fueled by soda?

A bottle rocket!

What toy do aliens like to play with?

Flying discs.

Why was the alien under arrest?

For shooting stars.

BOY: Look at that cool spaceship!

GIRL: It's out of this world!

Why do aliens live far away?

Alienation.

What do you get when you cross an alien with a red-winged blackbird?

A marsh-ian.

When is a reindeer a shooting star?

When it's Comet.

**HA HA HA HA HA
HA HA HA HA HA**

UFOS – UNIDENTIFIED FUNNY OBJECTS

What do get when you cross a Frisbee player and a horse rider?

Disc jockey!

BOY: Do you want to toss the Frisbee?

GIRL: Ultimately.

Knock-knock!

Who's there?

Boomerang.

Boomerang who?

Boomerang your doorbell!

What can you never tell a boomerang?

"Don't you ever come back!"

What do you get when you cross a music timer and a flying camera?

A metro-drone!

What do you call a hovering troll?

Gnome on a drone.

How do you spy an elf on a shelf?

With a gnome on a drone!

What do you call a solo hovering cell phone?

Lone drone phone.

What's a drone's favorite game?

I Spy!

Why are drone operators so boring?

Because they drone on and on and on.

When does a snowboarder become a bird?

When he catches some air.

NEIGHBOR: We're having a block party.
You should come.

SKYDIVER: Sure! I'll drop in.

Do hang gliders have hangnails?

HA HA HA HA HA HA HA HA HA

What did one hang glider say to another?

"Hang in there!"

Why did the hang glider never fly again?

He had too many hang-ups.

What delivery vehicle only flies one night a year?

Santa's sleigh!

TRAINER: Make sure your parachute is packed correctly.

STUDENT: I think mine is.

TRAINER: Don't jump to conclusions.

Skydivers are down-to-earth people.

What did the skydiver say when his cord wouldn't pull?

"Para-*shoot*!"

ON THE FLY

Why did the police put honey in the trap?
You can catch more flies with honey than vinegar.

Why do flies avoid computers?
They don't want to get caught in the World Wide Web!

What do you call a bug that loves high heels?
A shoe fly.

Zip it up: Are flies' flies ever open?

What newspaper do bugs read?
The Fly Paper!

What do you get when you cross a planet and flypaper?
A Venus flytrap!

What online classes do flies never take?
Webinars!

HA HA HA HA

HA HA HA HA HA
HA HA HA HA
HA HA HA HA HA

Why didn't any flies show up to the picnic?

Because they were serving shoofly pie.

What do you get when a fly lands on your phone?

A phone that's bugged!

What insect breathes fire?

A dragonfly!

What did the sewing-needle bug say when it tore a wing?

Darn it!

CAN YOU SAY THIS FIVE TIMES FAST?

Fast flies.

Flies would never hurt a fly.

Why did the fly stay away from the duck?

Because his feet were webbed.

Why do flies play it safe?

They don't like to get into sticky situations.

Overheard gossipers at an insect party:

"Oh, I'd love to be a fly on the wall."

Why did the fly go to the doctor?

Because it was a hoarse fly.

What has one seat and flies?

An outhouse!

What kind of fisherman needs a pilot's license?

The fly fisher!

FATHER: Son, where are you going with your fishing pole?

SON: To the dump.

FATHER: There are no fish there.

SON: That's okay. I'm going *fly*-fishing.

FLY: Peekaboo, I see you, and you, and you, and you, and you.

Are houseflies built by carpenter ants?

HA HA HA HA HA HA HA HA HA HA

HA HA HA HA

WINGLESS ZINGERS

What has wings but can't fly?

The White House.

Why should you avoid making deals with a kite salesperson?

Too many strings attached.

What did one kite say to another?

"Quit stringing me along."

How did Benjamin Franklin discover electricity?

His friend told him to go fly a kite!

What's the dandelion's favorite Bob Dylan song?

"Blowin' in the Wind."

Which actor is captivating to birds?

Nicolas Cage.

BOY: Can ovens fly?

DAD: No, son. Why do you ask?

BOY: Then why do they have pilot lights?

HA HA HA HA HA

What do you get when you cross a circus performer and a quadrilateral?

A flying trapezoid!

What do witches order at hotels?

Broom service!

What happened when the witch was mad?

She flew off the handle.

What has no wings but is caught on the fly?

A baseball!

Where do superheroes go on vacation?

Cape Canaveral.

Why did the hot-air balloon cut its strings?

It felt too tethered down.

Are hot-air balloonists full of hot air?

What did the teacher say to the graduating balloon pilot?

"The sky's the limit!"

HA HA HA HA

FAIRY FUNNY!

How does Peter Pan ring for room service?
With a Tinker Bell.

- -

Why will Peter Pan and Tinker Bell fly forever?
Because they live in Neverland.

- -

How do leprechauns cross the Irish Sea?
They take a fairy.

- -

What do you call a cow's magical godmother?
A dairy fairy.

- -

What do you get when you cross a shark
and a pixie?
A toothy fairy!

- -

What do you call a Gothic pixie?
Fairy Gothmother!

- -

What happened to Tinker Bell when she got
sprayed by a skunk?
She became Stinker Bell!

How do fairies buy things?

With Tinkerbills.

Why did J.M. Barrie's play about Neverland get bad reviews?

Peter got panned.

What do you call a sweet purple pixie?

Sugar Plum Fairy.

What do you find at the end of storybooks?

Fairy tails!

Knock-knock!

Who's there?

Dragon.

Dragon who?

Quit dragon your feet and come outside!

Why did the mythical creature go to the dentist?

It had dragon breath.

Knock-knock!

Who's there?

Fairy.

Fairy who?

I'm doing fairy well, thank you!

Why did the two pixies stop playing together?

They were fairy-weather friends.

Do tooth fairies ever lose their teeth?

What do you get when you cross an oxygen tank with a pixie?

An airy fairy!

Why did Cupid go to the doctor?

He had a broken heart.

Why did Cupid miss his target?

Love is blind.

Where does Cupid go to watch football games?

Arrowhead stadium.

After Cupid was let out of jail, he went on the straight and arrow.

How do you sweep up magic powder?

With a pixie duster.

CAN YOU SAY THIS FIVE TIMES FAST?

Cubic Cupid.

Why is Cupid so lovable?

He's all heart.

Where does Cupid go on vacation?

Loveland, Colorado!

HA HA HA HA
HA
HA HA HA HA
HA HA HA HA

HA HA HA HA HA HA HA HA

Why do Cupid's legs curve out?

Because he's bowlegged.

Knock-knock!

Who's there?

Cupid.

Cupid who?

Cupid the trash out?

What did one fairy say to the other?

"I haven't seen you in a fairy long time!"

GIRL: The tooth fairy collects canines.

BOY: She must have a lot of dogs!

What do old tooth fairies become?

Toothless fairies.

Where do fairies go when they die?

They cross over the rainbow bridge.

What did Cupid say when the chicken fell in love with the vulture?

"Oops!"

JOKES TO CROW ABOUT

What did the farmer say when he found blackbirds eating his corn?

I'll give them something to crow about.

What did the policeman arrest the gang of crows for?

Murder.

How did the policeman tie the blackbird's wings?

With Velcrow!

What did the blackbird have to do when it was proven wrong?

Eat crow.

What do you call a frightened blackbird?

Scarecrow.

HA HA

HA HA HA HA HA
HA HA HA HA HA
HA HA HA HA HA

Knock-knock!

Who's there?

Caws.

Caws who?

Caws I said so!

What do you think about a bird that loses all its flight feathers?

I have no o-pinion.

Knock-knock!

Who's there?

Raven.

Raven who?

I've been raven about your cooking!

MOTHER BIRD: I'm worried about my baby's weight.

DOCTOR: Why?

MOTHER BIRD: He eats like a bird.

Why did the bird go to the doctor?

Because it had the avian flu.

What's the raven's favorite singer?

Sheryl Crow.

- -

Why don't crows go near the La Brea Tar Pits?

They don't want to be tarred and feathered.

- -

How did the farmer grow a crop of crows instead of corn?

He planted birdseed!

- -

Where do ravens go on vacation?

Crow-atia!

- -

Why do crows sit on telephone wires?

They're trying to make phone caws.

- -

THAT'S ENTERTAINMENT!

What ballet show did the birds go see?

Swan Lake.

What James Bond spy movie stars birds?

Goldfincher.

Which hockey team has the most bird fans?

The Anaheim Ducks!

What's the mallard's favorite movie?

The Mighty Ducks!

What do you call a funny fowl?

A comedi-hen!

Why are turkeys always the drummers in bands?

They know how to use drumsticks!

What type of movies do baby chickens like?

Chick flicks.

What did Bugs Bunny say to the mallard?

"What's up, duck?"

What boxing division do birds compete in?

Featherweight.

What do you get when you cross the Blue Jays with the Red Sox?

Purple Jocks.

Why don't chickens make good baseball pitchers?

They always bawk.

Why don't chickens make good baseball umpires?

They only call fowls!

Who are the superheroes of the avian world?

Batman and Robin.

What do you call a superhero flying fish?

Cape Cod!

Where can you learn more about waterfowl?

Duckumentaries!

What is the songbird's favorite holiday movie?

How the Finch Stole Christmas!

Why did the jay go skiing?

It was a bluebird day!

HA HA HA HA HA HA HA HA

HA HA HA HA HA HA HA HA HA HA

Which flying mammals joined the circus?

The acro-bats.

What do you call a competition between fat birds?

A round-robin tournament!

PIGEON PUNS & LOVEY DOVEYS

How do pigeons like to see New York City?

From a bird's-eye view.

Are pigeons pigeon toed?

Why should you never invite stool pigeons to your celebrations?

Because they are party poopers.

How do doves from different countries speak to one another?

They use pigeon (pidgin) language.

Which pigeons always find their way back to their nests?

Homing pigeons!

Sign on pigeon's nest: Homing Sweet Homing.

What do you call a sweet group of doves?

Lovey-dovey covey.

Who did the dove fall in love with?

The girl nest door.

Take a seat: Do stool pigeons ever sit on couches?

What bird lays its eggs in the sand?

The turtledove!

Are turtledoves super-slow?

What time of day do doves like best?

Mourning.

HA HA HA HA HA
HA HA HA HA
HA HA HA HA HA

UNDER THE FEATHER

What bird chases lightning?

Thunderbird.

What did the bird say when the cloud predicted rain?

"Are you cirrus?"

How do you keep a bird out of the rain?

Give it an umbrella.

What did the chickadee say when the first snowstorm hit?

"*Brrrrrrrrd!*"

Why did the pheasant go to the doctor?

It was feeling under the feather.

What clothing has feathers but doesn't fly?

A down jacket.

How do snow angels celebrate their birthdays?

With snow blowers!

HA HA HA HA HA HA

What's the bird's favorite part of the news show?
The feather forecast!

What do you get when you thaw a macaw?
A chatty melt.

Why did the hawk check the weather forecast?
He wanted to know the *current* weather.

How do birds deliver letters in windy weather?
Via sail mail.

What do birds wear so they can ride air currents?
Thermal underwear.

What's a tornado's favorite donut?
   Funnel cakes.

What do you get when you cross a tropical storm
with a wetland bird?
   A hurri-crane.

What kind of insurance do wetland birds take out?
   Flood.

Why wasn't the oriole allowed to play
with matches?
   It was a firebird.

LOONEY LARKS

Which bird is a jokester?

A lark!

What brand of underwear do birds wear?

Fruit of the Loon.

What do you get when you cross an excited fan and heavy equipment?

A whooping crane!

Where do loons go to watch movies?

At the dive-in.

What kind of bird is easy to eat?

The swallow!

What bird can eat a bale of hay in one gulp?

A barn swallow!

Why do you never hear a ptarmigan going to the bathroom?

Because the *p* is silent!

HA HA HA HA HA

How do you know ptarmigans are masters of camouflage if you can't see them?

Which bird from Texas lived in the White House?
   Lady Bird Johnson.

What do you call an avian timepiece?
   A bird watch-er.

What reptilian dinosaur flew like a bird?
   Ptero-soar.

Knock-knock!
   Who's there?
Robin.
   Robin who?
Robin the bank!

What kind of bird can lift heavy objects?

A crane!

What do you get when you cross a redbird with a king?

A cardinal ruler.

Where do gobblers go for Thanksgiving?

To Turkey!

What bird is nest in line to the throne?

The kingfisher!

Knock-knock!

Who's there?

Wren.

Wren who?

Wren are we leaving?

HA HA HA HA
HA HA HA HA HA
HA HA HA HA
HA HA HA HA HA
HA HA HA HA

What do you call a bird traffic jam?

Grid-lark!

What kind of Christmas tree is filled with birds?

A flocked tree!

Why did the bird become a traitor?

Because it was a wren-egade!

What bird is always in trouble with the law?

A jailbird.

What is the robin's favorite kind of candy?

Gummy worms!

Knock-knock!

Who's there?

Pheasant.

Pheasant who?

Pheasant meeting you!

HA HA HA

How did the turkey cross the country?

He took the gravy train.

What mythical bird can you always get a rise out of?

The phoenix!

What do you get when you combine a starling with a fork?

A stork!

What was the blue bird arrested for?

Jaywalking!

Why wasn't Daffy Duck allowed in the band?

He always played Looney Tunes.

What did the hostess do when the stork requested dinner reservations on a busy night?

Put him on the wading list.

What did the bird buy on her shopping spree?

Wingtip shoes.

Why did the pterodactyl sing only twenty-five letters in the English alphabet?

The *p* was silent.

Why did the dog stay away from the beach?

He didn't want sand fleas.

What did the Little Bird Bakery serve?

Bay gulls and sweet tweets.

How did the bird get rich?

He knew how to tern a profit.

What do busy mama birds serve their babies when they don't have time to fetch worms?

Birds Eye® frozen dinners!

Why do birds make great lab partners?

They know how to use beakers.

What kind of birds are good at sneaking up on you?

Creepers!

What kind of chickens are blue?

Cocka-teals.

Where do new parents invest their money?

In the stork market!

What happened to the turkey when he retired?

His friends threw a party and roasted him.

HA HA HA HA

What's a bird's favorite snack?

Potato cheeps.

Why was there only one species at the bird-day party?

The invitation said, "Egrets only."

How did the author of this book come up with so many jokes?

She Winged it!

HA HA

ABOUT THE AUTHOR

Natasha Wing is a bestselling children's author who wrote *Bagel in Love*, a punny story about a dancing bagel, and *Lettuce Laugh*, a corny joke book of food jokes, both published by Sterling Children's Books. When things get tough her favorite phrase is "I'll just wing it!"